SQL and PL/SQL in Practice Series

Volume 2: Windowing for Analytics

Djoni Darmawikarta

Table of Contents

Preface

SQL for Analytics, the 2nd volume of the *SQL and PL/SQL in Practice* series, is for those who want to learn how to use the Oracle analytic functions. The analytic functions make it easier for us to write analytic queries.

This book is about the Oracle analytic functions that have windowing capabilities. You will learn analytic window, its clauses and options, by way of examples.

Book Examples

To learn the most out of this book, try the book examples. Set up your own Oracle database and SQL Developer tool to freely and safely try the examples.

You can download free of charge both the database and the tool from the Oracle website. Appendix A is your guide to install the software; Appendix B shows you how to particularly use SQL Developer to try the book examples.

The examples were tested well on Oracle Database 11g Expression Edition release 2 and SQL Developer version 4.

Note on Examples:

- The book examples are shown as SQL Developer screenshots.
- The number of rows of the table used in the examples is purposely small to facilitate your learning.
- Rows of the table might change from one example to another.

Prerequisite

You must have SQL working skill, particularly writing SQL queries. If you encounter SQL related difficulty in following this book, read the 1st volume of the book *SQL and PL/SQL in Practice series: Learning the Basics in No Time*.

Chapter 1: Window

In this chapter you will learn the basics of window. When you are done with the chapter, you will be able to answer the following three questions.

- What is a window?
- How do we specify a window?
- What are the two types of window?

A window is one or more ordered rows from which an aggregate value is computed by an analytic function. The window is specified in the analytic function.

Let's look at an example.

ROWS Window

Suppose we have a sales table as in Figure 1-1.

PRODUCT	QUANTITY
C	1
C++	2
Eclipse	3
MongoDB	4
MySQL	5
Oracle	6
PostgreSQL	7
R	8
RStudio	9
SQL	10

Figure 1-1 Sales table

The SQL statement in Example 1-1 uses an AVG analytic function.

```
SELECT product, quantity,
  AVG (quantity)
  OVER (ORDER BY product
  ROWS BETWEEN UNBOUNDED PRECEDING AND CURRENT ROW) caq
FROM sales;
```

Example 1-1 Query with AVG analytic function

The OVER (ORDER BY product ROWS BETWEEN UNBOUNDED PRECEDING AND CURRENT ROW) specifies the window of the AVG function.

■ The rows of the window are all rows that precede the current row and the current row itself. A current row is the row being computed for its average quantity. Each of the rows to be returned by the query has its own window.

■ The rows are ordered by product.

■ The AVG function computes the average of the quantities from the window rows. The average value returned by the function is stored as an output column we name caq. caq stands for <u>c</u>umulative <u>a</u>verage of <u>q</u>uantities.

Cumulative computation

As mentioned earlier, an analytic function computes an aggregate value from the window rows.

Here are, for example, the caq computations of the first three rows and the last row.

■ The 1st row (C) does not have any preceding row; hence its window is only its row. As its quantity = 1, its caq is $1 / 1 = 1$.

PRODUCT	QUANTITY	CAQ
C	1	1
C++	2	1.5
Eclipse	3	2
MongoDB	4	2.5
MySQL	5	3
Oracle	6	3.5
PostgreSQL	7	4
R	8	4.5
RStudio	9	5
SQL	10	5.5

current window

current row

■ The 2nd row (C++) has one preceding row, the C row; hence its window is the first and second rows. The caq is $(1 + 2)/2 = 1.5$.

4

PRODUCT	QUANTITY	CAQ
C	1	1
C++	2	1.5
Eclipse	3	2
MongoDB	4	2.5
MySQL	5	3
Oracle	6	3.5
PostgreSQL	7	4
R	8	4.5
RStudio	9	5
SQL	10	5.5

current window — current row

- The 3rd row (Eclipse) has two preceding rows (the C and C++ rows, which have quantity = 1 and 2 respectively), hence its window is the two rows and itself. Its caq is $(1 + 2 + 3)/3 = 2$.

PRODUCT	QUANTITY	CAQ
C	1	1
C++	2	1.5
Eclipse	3	2
MongoDB	4	2.5
MySQL	5	3
Oracle	6	3.5
PostgreSQL	7	4
R	8	4.5
RStudio	9	5
SQL	10	5.5

current window — current row

- The last row (SQL)'s window is all ten rows. Its caq is the sum of all quantities divided by 10 = 5.5.

PRODUCT	QUANTITY	CAQ
C	1	1
C++	2	1.5
Eclipse	3	2
MongoDB	4	2.5
MySQL	5	3
Oracle	6	3.5
PostgreSQL	7	4
R	8	4.5
RStudio	9	5
SQL	10	5.5

current window — current row

Table 1-1 outlines the windows and the caq computation of every one of the ten rows.

Current Row	Start Row	End Row	Number of Rows	Sum of Quantities	caq = Sum of Quantities/ Number of Rows
C	1	1	1	1	1
C++	1	2	2	(1+2) = 3	3 / 2 = 1.5
Eclipse	1	3	3	(1+2+3) = 6	6 / 3 = 2
MongoDB	1	4	4	(1+2+3+4) = 10	10 / 4 = 2.5
MySQL	1	5	5	(1+2+3+4+5) = 15	15 / 5 =3
Oracle	1	6	6	(1+2+3+4+5+6) = 21	21 / 6 = 3.5
PostgreSQL	1	7	7	(1+2+3+4+5+6+7) = 28	28 / 7 = 4
R	1	8	8	(1+2+3+4+5+6+7+8) = 36	36 / 8 = 4.5
RStudio	1	9	9	(1+2+3+4+5+6+7+8+9) = 45	45 / 9 = 5
SQL	1	10	10	(1+2+3+4+5+6+7+8+9+10) = 55	55 / 10 = 5.5

Table 1-1 caq computation of every row

RANGE Window

```
OVER(ORDER BY product ROWS …
```

Instead of ROWS, you can apply RANGE.

```
OVER(ORDER BY product RANGE …
```

While ROWS specifies rows directly, RANGE specifies rows by way of values. Hence, ROWS is known as identifying *physical* rows (the window is therefore referred to as a physical window); while RANGE as identifying *logical* rows (the window is therefore referred to as a logical window)

The values used by the RANGE to specify the window rows are the values of the ORDER BY argument, which in our case is *product*.

Let's look at an example to clarify.

```
SELECT product,
  quantity,
  AVG(quantity)
  OVER(ORDER BY product
  RANGE BETWEEN UNBOUNDED PRECEDING
  AND CURRENT ROW) cag
FROM sales;
```

Example 1-2 RANGE window

The query in Example 1-2 uses RANGE. Its output is the same as the output of the query in Example 1-1.

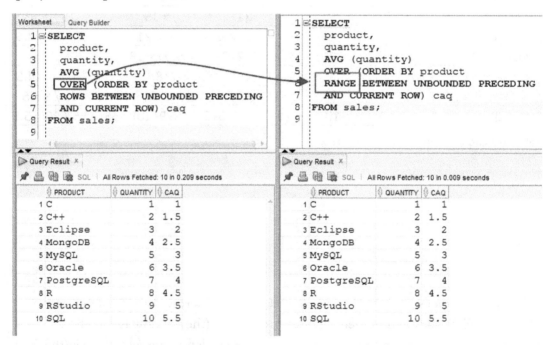

Figure 1-2 RANGE's output is the same as ROW's

What if the sales table has duplicate rows, rows with the same product?

In the following example the sales table has two C rows and two Oracle rows. The query with ROWS produces the same output as before as ROWS refers to physical rows. But, RANGE produces a different caq, as RANGE refers to the value, i.e. the product.

For the 1st row, the current row's value is C. Its current window is all preceding rows (which it has none) and C rows (the 1st and 2nd rows). Hence, the function computes the average from the quantities of the first two rows = $(1 + 2) / 2 = 1.5$.

The window of the 2nd row is also the C rows, hence its caq is the same = 1.5.

Let's look at the other duplicates, the 5th and 6th rows. The value of the 5th row is Oracle. Its current window is the two Oracle rows and all their preceding rows. The caq is $((1+2+3+4) + (5+6)) / 6 = 3.5$. The 6th row's window is the same as the 5th row's, hence its caq is also the same, 3.5.

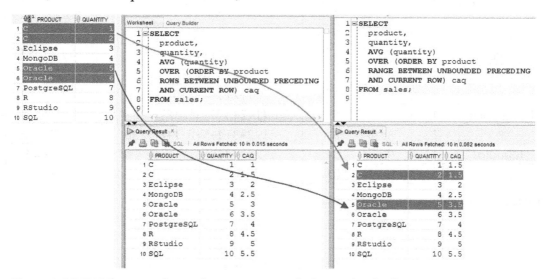

Figure 1-3 RANGE's output is not the same as ROW's due to the duplicate rows

Table 1-2 summarizes the caq computation of every one of the ten rows.

Current Window					caq = Sum of Quantities/ Number of Rows
Current Row	Start Row	End Row	Number of Rows	Sum of Quantities	
C	1	2	2	(1+2) = 3	3 / 2 = 1.5
C	1	2	2	(1+2) = 3	3 / 2 = 1.5
Eclipse	1	3	3	(1+2+3) = 6	6 / 3 = 2
MongoDB	1	4	4	(1+2+3+4) = 10	10 / 4 = 2.5
Oracle	1	6	6	(1+2+3+4+5+6) = 21	21 / 6 =3.5
Oracle	1	6	6	(1+2+3+4+5+6) = 21	21 / 6 = 3.5
PostgreSQL	1	7	7	(1+2+3+4+5+6+7) = 28	28 / 7 = 4
R	1	8	8	(1+2+3+4+5+6+7+8) = 36	36 / 8 = 4.5
RStudio	1	9	9	(1+2+3+4+5+6+7+8+9) = 45	45 / 9 = 5
SQL	1	10	10	(1+2+3+4+5+6+7+8+9+10) = 55	55 / 10 = 5.5

Table 1-2 caq computation of every row

Dynamic

You might have recognized from the examples that window is dynamic.

- It slides along with its current row
- Its size (number of rows) changes. In the examples:
  - With ROWS, the window size grows incrementally by one with every subsequent row regardless any duplicate rows. The change is constant.
  - With RANGE the window size depends on the number of duplicates. Within duplicate rows, the window size does not change. Moving from duplicate rows to the next, the window size changes, and the increment depends on the size of the duplicates. The change is not always constant.

What is Next?

ROWS or RANGE BETWEEN UNBOUNDED PRECEDING AND CURRENT ROW are not the only options for specifying window. In the next chapter, Chapter 2, you will learn the various options for specifying window.

Chapter 2: Window Clause

The focus of Chapter 1 is what a window is. In this chapter you will learn the various options for specifying window.

An analytic function can have one to three clauses. The syntax of analytic function is as follows.

```
analytic_function ([arguments]) OVER (
[partition_clause] [order_clause [window_clause]])
```

In the examples of Chapter 1, the **ORDER BY product ROWS BETWEEN UNBOUNDED PRECEDING AND CURRENT ROW** of the window specification **OVER (ORDER BY product ROWS BETWEEN UNBOUNDED PRECEDING AND CURRENT ROW)** is the order_clause and window_clause parts of the syntax.

The focus of this chapter is the window_clause.

The following window_clause syntax shows the possible options.

```
{ROWS | RANGE}
BETWEEN
  {UNBOUNDED PRECEDING
  | CURRENT ROW                                      start
  | start expression {PRECEDING | FOLLOWING}
  }
AND
  {UNBOUNDED FOLLOWING
  | CURRENT ROW                                      end
  | end expression {PRECEDING | FOLLOWING}
  }
```

Please observe the following two syntax notations.

■ One of the options within { } must be used.
■ One of the options separated by | must be used.

UNBOUNDED and CURRENT ROW options

Table 2-1 shows four window specifications you can specify using the UNBOUNDED and CURRENT ROW options and their resulting windows.

Option	Window
BETWEEN CURRENT ROW AND CURRENT ROW	Current row only
BETWEEN CURRENT ROW AND UNBOUNDED FOLLOWING	Current row and all rows following current row
BETWEEN UNBOUNDED PRECEDING AND CURRENT ROW	All rows preceding current row and the current row
BETWEEN UNBOUNDED PRECEDING AND UNBOUNDED FOLLOWING	All rows

Table 2-1 CURRENT ROW – UNBOUNDED window specifications

We already use the "ROWS BETWEEN UNBOUNDED PRECEDING AND CURRENT ROW" in the examples of Chapter 1. This is *the default* window clause. The default window for RANGE is the same.

Example 2-1 does not have any window clause. It produces the same output as Example 1-1.

```
SELECT product, quantity,
  AVG (quantity)
  OVER (ORDER BY product) caq
FROM sales;
```

Example 2-1 Default Window (no window clause)

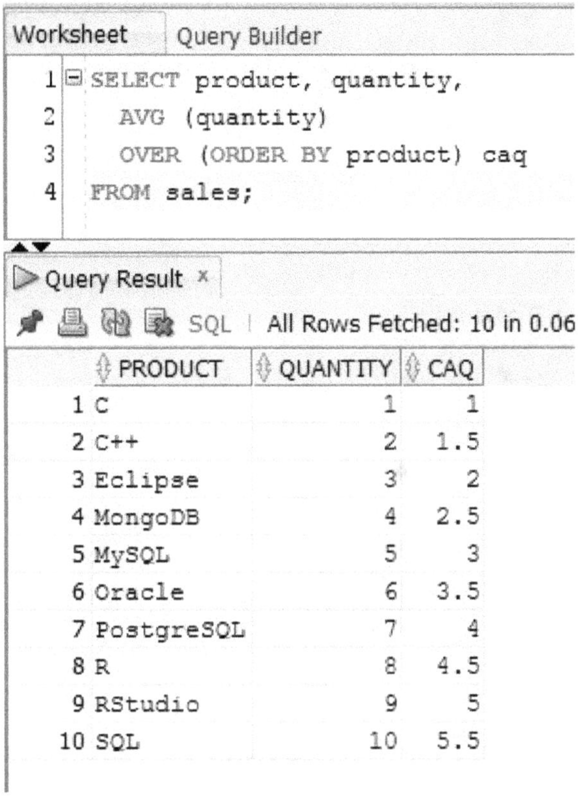

Figure 2-1 Output of Example 2-1 Default Window (no window clause)

ROWS BETWEEN CURRENT ROW AND CURRENT ROW is not interesting, as its window is always one row, only the current row itself as shown next. The caq is the quantity of the current row.

```
SELECT product, quantity,
  AVG (quantity)
  OVER (ORDER BY product
  ROWS BETWEEN CURRENT ROW AND CURRENT ROW) caq
FROM sales;
```

Example 2-2 ROWS CURRENT ROW

```
Worksheet    Query Builder
1⊟ SELECT product, quantity,
2    AVG (quantity)
3    OVER (ORDER BY product
4    ROWS BETWEEN CURRENT ROW AND CURRENT ROW) caq
5  FROM sales;
```

▷ Query Result ✕

🔧 🖨 🔃 🔳 SQL │ All Rows Fetched: 12 in 0 seconds

	PRODUCT	QUANTITY	CAQ
1	C	3	3
2	C	1	1
3	C++	2	2
4	Eclipse	3	3
5	MongoDB	4	4
6	MySQL	5	5
7	Oracle	4	4
8	Oracle	6	6
9	PostgreSQL	7	7
10	R	8	8
11	RStudio	9	9
12	SQL	10	10

Figure 2-2 Output of Example 2-2

But, **RANGE** BETWEEN CURRRENT ROW AND CURRENT ROW can be interesting. The window of the duplicates are the duplicate rows. Their caq's are the same, their average.

```
SELECT product, quantity,
  AVG (quantity)
  OVER (ORDER BY product
  RANGE BETWEEN CURRENT ROW AND CURRENT ROW) caq
FROM sales;
```

Example 2-2 RANGE CURRENT ROW

```
Worksheet    Query Builder
  1 ⊟ SELECT product, quantity,
  2     AVG (quantity)
  3     OVER (ORDER BY product
  4       RANGE BETWEEN CURRENT ROW AND CURRENT ROW) caq
  5   FROM sales;
```

▷ Query Result ×

📌 🖨 🏷 🏷 SQL | All Rows Fetched: 12 in 0 seconds

	PRODUCT	QUANTITY	CAQ
1	C	3	2
2	C	1	2
3	C++	2	2
4	Eclipse	3	3
5	MongoDB	4	4
6	MySQL	5	5
7	Oracle	4	5
8	Oracle	6	5
9	PostgreSQL	7	7
10	R	8	8
11	RStudio	9	9
12	SQL	10	10

Figure 2-3 Output of Example 2-3

Start and end expressions options

The start and end expression is an SQL expression. It can simply be a constant, or a complex computation involving constants, columns, and functions.

The start expression and end expression are the boundaries of a window. The ROWS BETWEEN 2 PRECEDING AND 1 FOLLOWING in Example 2-3 means the window boundaries are 2nd row preceding the current row and the 1st row following the current row. The boundary rows are included in the window.

Here are some examples of boundaries.

- For the first row, the window boundary is itself (as there's no preceding row) and the second row, hence its maq $= (3 +1)/2 = 2$.
- For the second row, the window boundaries are the first row and the third row, hence its maq $= (3 + 1 + 2) / 3 = 2$.

- For the third row, the window boundaries are the first row and the fourth row, hence its maq = (3+1+2+3) / 4 =2.25.

```
SELECT
  product,
  quantity,
  AVG (quantity)
  OVER (ORDER BY product
  ROWS BETWEEN
  2 PRECEDING AND 1 FOLLOWING) caq
FROM sales;
```

Example 2-3 Start and End Expressions

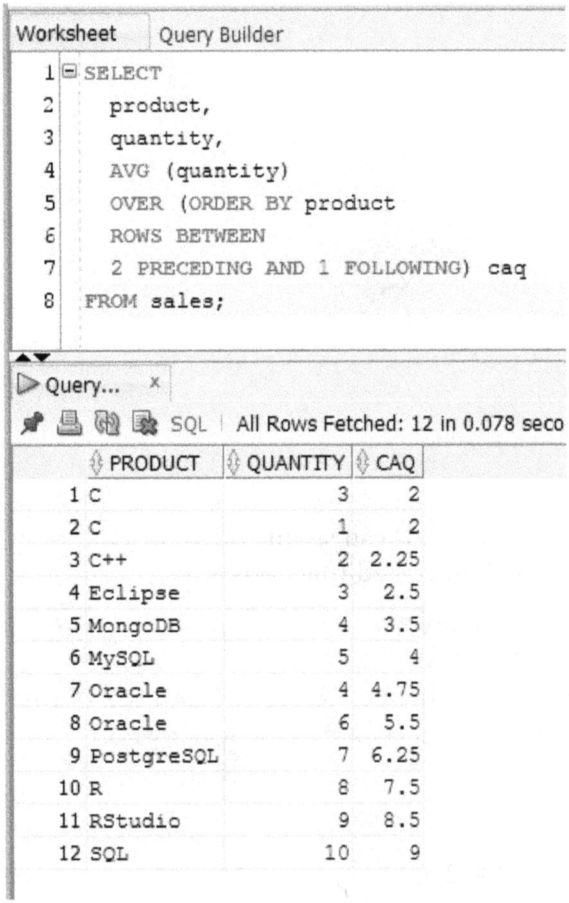

	PRODUCT	QUANTITY	CAQ
1	C	3	2
2	C	1	2
3	C++	2	2.25
4	Eclipse	3	2.5
5	MongoDB	4	3.5
6	MySQL	5	4
7	Oracle	4	4.75
8	Oracle	6	5.5
9	PostgreSQL	7	6.25
10	R	8	7.5
11	RStudio	9	8.5
12	SQL	10	9

Figure 2-3 Start and End Expressions

Start and end expressions give you flexibility in specifying window, but you must observe the followings.

- For ROWS, expression must be positive numeric. Remember that the expressions identify physical rows.
- For RANGE, expression must be positive numeric or positive date/time interval. Remember that you use RANGE to specify logical window. The window rows are identified by way of value, the value of the ORDER BY argument. In all our examples so far, the argument is product, which is neither numeric nor date/time data type; hence, it is not a valid argument.
- Start expression must be <= end expression.
- You can combine start or end expression with the UNBOUNDED or CURRENT ROW.

Limited Cumulative

You have seen that the use of **OVER (ROWS BETWEEN UNBOUNDED PRECEDING AND CURRENT ROW)** window specification is for computing cumulative aggregation.

You can use a start expression to limit the number of preceding rows. In Example 2-4 the **OVER (ROWS BETWEEN 2 PRECEDING AND CURRENT ROW)** limits the number of preceding rows to 2.

```
SELECT
  product,
  quantity,
  AVG (quantity)
  OVER (ORDER BY product
  ROWS BETWEEN
  2 PRECEDING AND CURRENT ROW) caq
FROM sales;
```

Example 2-4 Limited Cumulative

```
Worksheet | Query Builder
1 □ SELECT
2     product,
3     quantity,
4     AVG (quantity)
5     OVER (ORDER BY product
6     ROWS BETWEEN
7     2 PRECEDING AND CURRENT ROW) caq
8   FROM sales;
```

▲▼

Query Result ×

📌 🖨 🔂 🔃 SQL | All Rows Fetched: 12 in 0 seconds

PRODUCT	QUANTITY	CAQ
1 C	3	3
2 C	1	2
3 C++	2	2
4 Eclipse	3	2
5 MongoDB	4	3
6 MySQL	5	4
7 Oracle	4	4.33333333333333333333333333333333333333
8 Oracle	6	5
9 PostgreSQL	7	5.66666666666666666666666666666666666667
10 R	8	7
11 RStudio	9	8
12 SQL	10	9

Figure 2-4 Output of limited cumulative

The following query with RANGE fails because the argument of the ORDER BY is not numeric or time data type.

```
SELECT
  product,
  quantity,
  AVG (quantity)
  OVER (ORDER BY product
 RANGE BETWEEN
  2 PRECEDING AND CURRENT ROW) caq
FROM sales;
```

Example 2-5 Non numeric on the order by

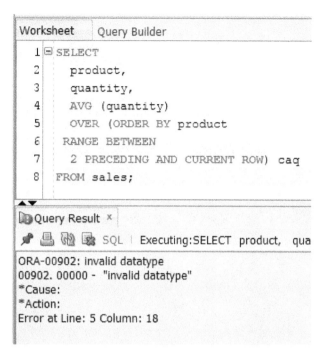

Figure 2-5 Failure on non-numeric order by

Moving Average

The following query with RANGE and ORDER BY sales_date is good, as the sales_date is a date data type. The AVG function returns a 3-days moving average of quantities.

```
SELECT
  product,
  quantity,
  AVG (quantity)
  OVER (ORDER BY sales_date
 RANGE BETWEEN
  2 PRECEDING AND CURRENT ROW) maq
FROM sales;
```

Example 2-6 Moving average

```
Worksheet    Query Builder
  1 ⊟ SELECT
  2     product, sales_date,
  3     quantity,
  4     AVG (quantity)
  5     OVER (ORDER BY sales_date
  6   RANGE BETWEEN
  7     2 PRECEDING AND CURRENT ROW) maq
  8   FROM sales;
```

▶ Query Result ×

📌 🖨 🐾 📇 SQL │ All Rows Fetched: 12 in 0.016 seconds

	PRODUCT	SALES_DATE	QUANTITY	MAQ
1	C	04-JUN-16	3	3
2	MySQL	04-JUN-16	5	3
3	C	04-JUN-16	1	3
4	Eclipse	05-JUN-16	3	3
5	R	07-JUN-16	8	5.375
6	RStudio	07-JUN-16	9	5.375
7	PostgreSQL	07-JUN-16	7	5.375
8	Oracle	07-JUN-16	4	5.375
9	MongoDB	07-JUN-16	4	5.375
10	C++	07-JUN-16	2	5.375
11	Oracle	07-JUN-16	6	5.375
12	SQL	08-JUN-16	10	6.25

Figure 2-6 Moving average over time (sales date)

Centered

Example 2-7 using the same value of start and end expressions producing centered cumulative average. The window is always five rows; the 3rd row is always the middle (center) row of the five rows.

```
SELECT
  product,
  quantity,
  AVG (quantity)
  OVER (ORDER BY product
  ROWS BETWEEN
```

```
  2 PRECEDING AND 2 FOLLOWING) caq
FROM sales;
```

Example 2-7 Centered cumulative average

Empty Window

A window can be empty, it does not have any row as demonstrated in Example … The first row does not have any preceding row, and hence its window is an empty window. Its caq hence is null.

In Example 2-8 the window is between the 4th preceding row and the 2nd preceding row; hence the window for the second row is also empty.

```
SELECT
  product,
  quantity,
  AVG (quantity)
  OVER (ORDER BY product
  ROWS BETWEEN 4 PRECEDING AND 2 PRECEDING) maq
FROM sales;
```

Example 2-8 Empty window

```
Worksheet    Query Builder
1 ⊟ SELECT
2     product,
3     quantity,
4     AVG (quantity)
5     OVER (ORDER BY product
6     ROWS BETWEEN 4 PRECEDING AND 2 PRECEDING) maq
7   FROM sales;
```

▲▼

▷ Query Result ×

📌 🖨 🔁 📑 SQL │ All Rows Fetched: 12 in 0 seconds

	PRODUCT	QUANTITY	MAQ
1	C	3	(null)
2	C	1	(null)
3	C++	2	3
4	Eclipse	3	2
5	MongoDB	4	2
6	MySQL	5	2
7	Oracle	4	3
8	Oracle	6	4
9	PostgreSQL	7	4.3333333333333333333333333333333333333333
10	R	8	5
11	RStudio	9	5.6666666666666666666666666666666666666667
12	SQL	10	7

Figure 2-7 Empty windows

Non Integer

The start and end expressions do not need to be integer. But there is no such thing as non-integer number of rows; for example, 1.1 rows do not make sense.

So, ROWS BETWEEN 1.1 PRECEDING AND 3.9 FOLLOWING translates to BETWEEN 2 PRECEDING AND 3 FOLLOWING. The start expression is rounded up to the next integer and the end expression is rounded down to the previous integer.

```
SELECT product, quantity,
  AVG(quantity)
```

```
  OVER(ORDER BY product
  ROWS BETWEEN 1.1 preceding AND 3.9 FOLLOWING) caq
FROM sales;
```

Example 2-9 Non integer

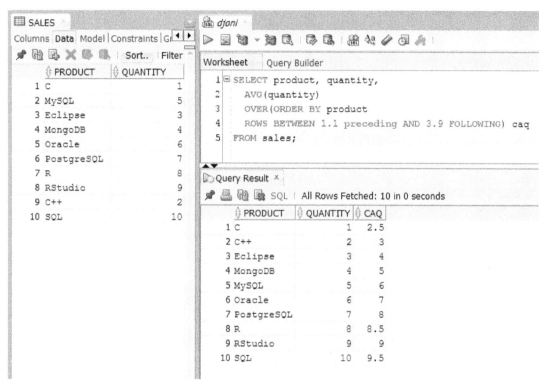

Figure 2-8 Non integer

What is Next?

By definition a window is one or more ordered rows. The ordering is achieved by the ORDER BY clause, which is mandatory. The next chapter covers this clause in details.

Chapter 3: Order Clause

A window clause must be preceded by an ORDER BY clause.

Here is the analytic function syntax again.

```
analytic_function ([arguments]) OVER (
[partition_clause] [order_clause [window_clause]])
```

You will learn the optional partition clause in Chapter 4.

And, here is the syntax of the order clause.

```
ORDER BY {expr | position | column_alias} [ASC | DESC]
[NULLS FIRST | NULLS LAST]
  [, {expr | position | column_alias} [ASC | DESC]
    [NULLS FIRST | NULLS LAST]
  ]...
```

The order clause orders (sorts) the window rows.

- Ascending is the default. Override the default by explicitly specifying DESC.
- Null value is considered the biggest by default. Use the NULLS FIRST or NULLS LAST if you need to override this Null default (the biggest).

Descending

In Examples 3-1 we order the rows descending: rows having higher unit price comes
before those having lower unit price.

```
SELECT product,
  category,
  unit_price,
  quantity,
  AVG(quantity)
  OVER(PARTITION BY category
  ORDER BY unit_price DESC
  ROWS BETWEEN UNBOUNDED PRECEDING AND CURRENT ROW) avg_qty
FROM sales;
```

Example 3-1 Descending on unit price

```
Worksheet    Query Builder
1 ⊟SELECT product,
2 |   category,
3 |   unit_price,
4 |   quantity,
5 |   AVG(quantity)
6 |   OVER(PARTITION BY category
7 |   ORDER BY unit_price DESC
8 |   ROWS BETWEEN UNBOUNDED PRECEDING AND CURRENT ROW) avg_qty
9 |FROM sales;
```

> Query Result ×
SQL | All Rows Fetched: 10 in 0.047 seconds

	PRODUCT	CATEGORY	UNIT_PRICE	QUANTITY	AVG_QTY
1	PostgreSQL	Database	7	7	
2	MongoDB	Database	6	4	
3	Oracle	Database	5	6	5.66666666666666666666
4	MySQL	Database	4	5	
5	RStudio	IDE	9	9	
6	Eclipse	IDE	3	3	
7	SQL	Language	10	10	
8	C++	Language	8	2	
9	R	Language	2	8	6.66666666666666666666
10	C	Language	1	1	

Figure 3-1 Descending on unit price

ORDER BY Non Numeric

```
SELECT product,
  category,
  quantity,
  AVG(quantity) OVER(ORDER BY product ROWS BETWEEN 1 preceding AND 1
      FOLLOWING
  ) avg_qty
FROM sales;
```

Example 3-2 ORDER BY non-numeric (product)

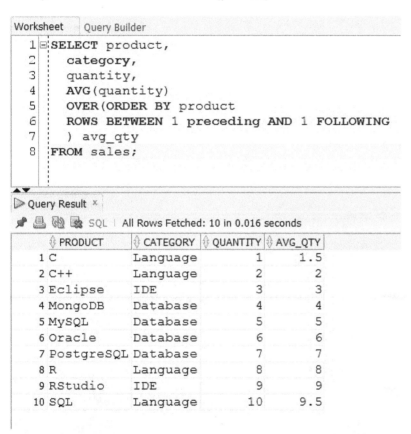

Figure 3-2 ORDER BY non-numeric (product)

Deterministic vs. Non-deterministic

A function is deterministic if, for the same arguments, it always returns the same result.

- If you use RANGE on analytic functions, the functions are deterministic.
- If you use ROWS, the analytic functions are deterministic only if the ORDER BY expressions list achieves unique ordering.

In the following examples the ORDER BY expression in the analytic clause, the sales date column, is not unique.

```
SELECT product,
  category,
  quantity,
  sales_date,
  ROUND( AVG(quantity)
  over (partition BY category
  order by sales_date
  rows BETWEEN 1 preceding AND 2 following) ,2 ) avg_qty
FROM (select * from sales
ORDER BY category)
order by category, product;
```

Example 3-3 Non unique sales date

	PRODUCT	CATEGORY	SALES_DATE	QUANTITY
1	Oracle	Database	13-JUN-16	7
2	MongoDB	Database	04-JUN-16	4
3	PostgreSQL	Database	04-JUN-16	1
4	MySQL	Database	05-JUN-16	4
5	Eclipse	IDE	05-JUN-16	1
6	RStudio	IDE	07-JUN-16	2
7	C++	Language	05-JUN-16	4
8	C	Language	04-JUN-16	5
9	R	Language	06-JUN-16	6
10	SQL	Language	17-JUN-16	5

Figure 3-3 Non unique sales date

In the examples the AVG function is not deterministic. When we change the ORDER BY of the source rows (the rows returned by the subquery SELECT statement) from ascending to descending (DESC), some rows get different AVG_QTY; for example, the avg_qty's of MySQL, MongoDB, and PostgreSQL, are different.

```
SELECT product,
  category,
  quantity,
  sales_date,
  ROUND( AVG(quantity)
  over (partition BY category
  order by sales_date
  rows BETWEEN 1 preceding AND 2 following) ,2 ) avg_qty
FROM (select * from sales
ORDER BY category DESC)
order by category, product;
```

Example 3-4 Non-deterministic

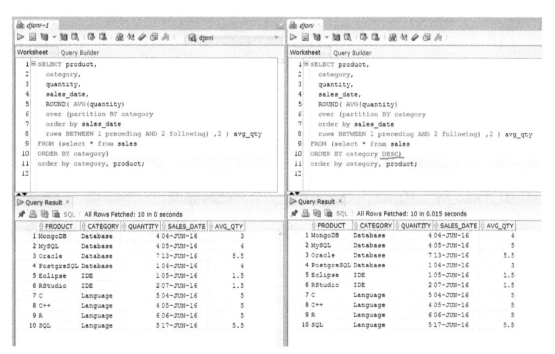

Figure 3-4 Non unique sales date

In the following two examples, we make the function's ORDER BY unique by adding product. Now regardless the row orders of the SELECT statement, the avg_qty's of the rows are the same.

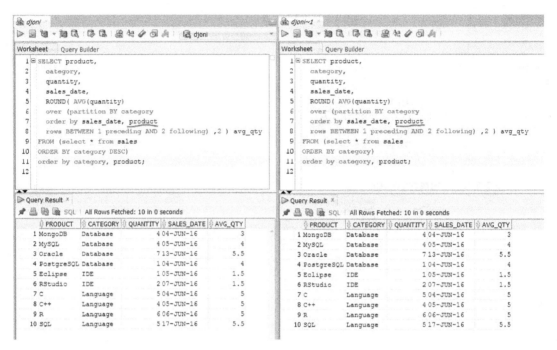

Figure 3-5 Deterministic

Multiple expressions in the ORDER BY clause

With the CURRENT ROW and se combinations, the ORDER BY clause can have more than one expression.

```
SELECT product,
  sales_date,
  quantity,
  SUM (quantity)
  OVER (
  ORDER BY product, sales_date
  RANGE BETWEEN UNBOUNDED PRECEDING AND CURRENT ROW) AS caq
FROM sales;
```

Example 3-5 Order by with multiple expressions

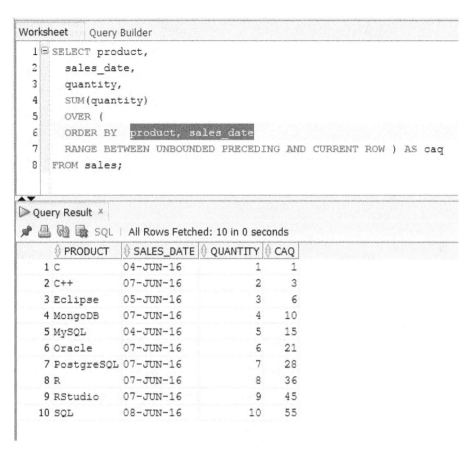

Figure 3-6 Order by with multiple expressions

With ROWS you can apply any combination of the CURRENT ROW or UNBOUNDED with the expression as long as you observe the above three points.

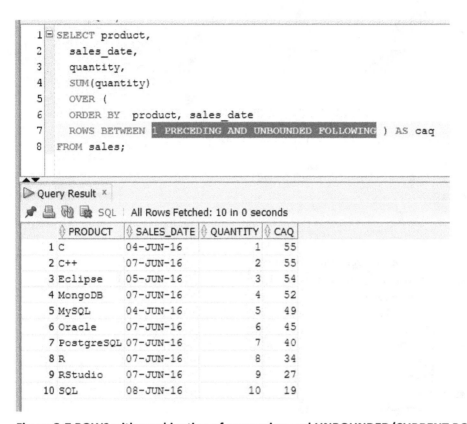

```
1 □ SELECT product,
2      sales_date,
3      quantity,
4      SUM(quantity)
5      OVER (
6      ORDER BY  product, sales_date
7      ROWS BETWEEN 1 PRECEDING AND UNBOUNDED FOLLOWING ) AS caq
8   FROM sales;
```

Query Result ×

SQL | All Rows Fetched: 10 in 0 seconds

	PRODUCT	SALES_DATE	QUANTITY	CAQ
1	C	04-JUN-16	1	55
2	C++	07-JUN-16	2	55
3	Eclipse	05-JUN-16	3	54
4	MongoDB	07-JUN-16	4	52
5	MySQL	04-JUN-16	5	49
6	Oracle	07-JUN-16	6	45
7	PostgreSQL	07-JUN-16	7	40
8	R	07-JUN-16	8	34
9	RStudio	07-JUN-16	9	27
10	SQL	08-JUN-16	10	19

Figure 3-7 ROWS with combination of expression and UNBOUNDED/CURRENT ROW

But not with RANGE, you cannot mix them.

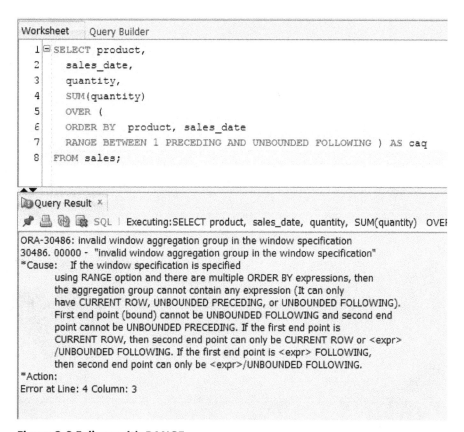

Figure 3-8 Failure with RANGE

What is Next?

A partition is a boundary: A window of a partition does not consider any row in other partitions. In a nutshell, using partition you can exercise more control on your windowing.

You will learn the PARTITION BY clause in the next chapter.

Chapter 4: Partition Clause

As mentioned in Chapter 2, an analytic function can have three clauses. We have covered the window clause and the order clause. In this Chapter you will learn the partition clause.

Here is the analytic function syntax again showing the three clauses.

```
Analytic function ([arguments])
OVER ([partition clause] [order clause [window clause]])
```

A partition clause is optional. If it is present, the partition clause must be before the order clause.

Partition

A partition is a boundary: A window of a partition does not consider any row in other partitions.

The syntax of the partition clause is:

```
PARTITION BY {expression [, expression]...
              | (expression [, expression]...)}
```

- Expression is an SQL expression, which can be a constant, a column, or anything more complex, such as a subquery. See Example 4-3 below.
- A PARTITION BY can have multiple expressions. See Example 4-2 below.
- The { }, not to be written in the query, indicates that one of the enclosed options must be selected, meaning you choose not to enclose or to enclose the expressions in ( ) grouping expressions for readability.
- You don't write the { }, [ ], ( ), and the | in the SQL statement.

    Let's look at various examples.

Example 4-1 does not explicitly have a window clause. The default window BETWEEN UNBOUNDED PRECEDING AND CURRENT ROW is in effect as soon as a valid ORDER BY is present.

When a different partition starts its first row's window does not have any preceding row, as no row in any other partition is considered.

```
SELECT
  product, category, quantity,
  AVG(quantity)
  OVER(PARTITION BY category
  ORDER BY product) aq
FROM
  sales;
```

Example 4-1 Default window

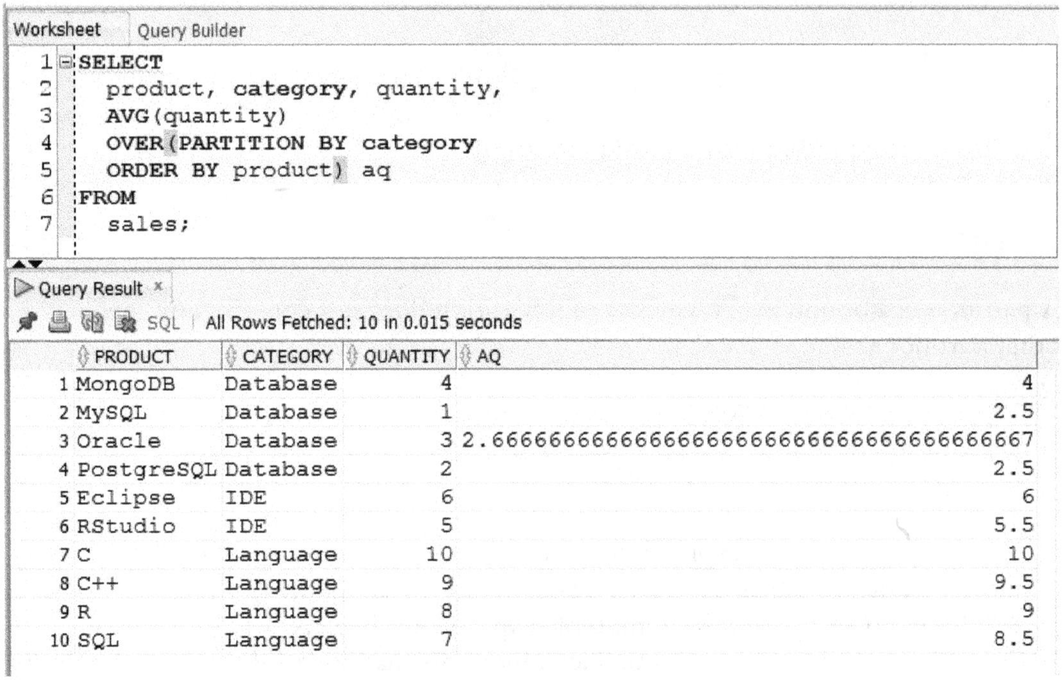

```
Worksheet   Query Builder
  1 ⊟SELECT
  2 |   product, category, quantity,
  3 |   AVG(quantity)
  4 |   OVER(PARTITION BY category
  5 |   ORDER BY product) aq
  6 |FROM
  7 |   sales;
```

> Query Result ×
📌 🖨 📑 📑 SQL | All Rows Fetched: 10 in 0.015 seconds

	PRODUCT	CATEGORY	QUANTITY	AQ
1	MongoDB	Database	4	4
2	MySQL	Database	1	2.5
3	Oracle	Database	3	2.6666666666666666666666666666666666666667
4	PostgreSQL	Database	2	2.5
5	Eclipse	IDE	6	6
6	RStudio	IDE	5	5.5
7	C	Language	10	10
8	C++	Language	9	9.5
9	R	Language	8	9
10	SQL	Language	7	8.5

Figure 4-1 Default window in effect

Multiple Expressions

In Example 4-2 the PARTITION BY has two expressions. The boundary is category and sales date; it is no longer just category, resulting in eight partitions.

```
Worksheet    Query Builder
  1 ⊟ SELECT
  2 │    product, category, sales_date, quantity,
  3 │    AVG(quantity)
  4 │    OVER(PARTITION BY category, sales_date
  5 │    ORDER BY product) aq
  6 │ FROM
  7 │    sales;
```

Query Result ×

📌 🖨 🔄 🔃 SQL | All Rows Fetched: 10 in 0.109 seconds

	PRODUCT	CATEGORY	SALES_DATE	QUANTITY	AQ
1	MySQL	Database	16-06-04	1	1
2	PostgreSQL	Database	16-06-04	2	1.5
3	Oracle	Database	16-06-05	3	3
4	MongoDB	Database	16-06-09	4	4
5	Eclipse	IDE	16-06-05	6	6
6	RStudio	IDE	16-06-05	5	5.5
7	C	Language	16-06-04	10	10
8	R	Language	16-06-05	8	8
9	C++	Language	16-06-07	9	9
10	SQL	Language	16-06-10	7	7

Figure 4-2 Multiple expressions

More Complex Partition

In Example 4-3, the expression of the partition clause is a correlated subquery.

```
SELECT
  product, quantity,
  AVG(quantity)
  OVER(PARTITION BY
  (SELECT price
  FROM product p WHERE p.product=s.product)
  ORDER BY product) aq
FROM
  sales s;
```

Example 4-3 Subquery expression

36

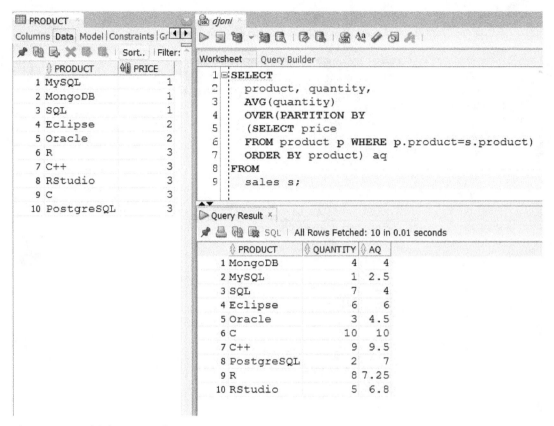

Figure 4-3 Multiple expressions

What is Next?

Having learned the three clauses to specify window, you will next look into how queries use analytic function.

Chapter 5: Analytic Function

Now that you have learned the clauses of analytic function, you will in this chapter learn the analytic function itself.

For your convenience, here is again the syntax of analytic function.

```
analytic_function ([arguments]) OVER (
[partition_clause] [order_clause [window_clause]])
```

In this chapter you will learn the following topics:

- Multiple functions
- Nesting functions
- Source rows
- Ordering output rows
- Analytic function in the query's order clause

The arguments are not the same for all analytic functions. So we will in the next chapter (Chapter 6), where you will learn each of the analytic functions, cover the arguments.

Multiple Functions

The queries of all previous examples have one analytic function in their select list. The following example (Example 5-1) has two analytic functions: one AVG and one COUNT.

```
SELECT
  product, sales_date, quantity,
  AVG(quantity) OVER(ORDER BY product DESC) caq,
  COUNT (*) OVER(ORDER BY sales_date
  RANGE BETWEEN 1 PRECEDING
  AND CURRENT ROW) cnt
FROM sales;
```

Example 5-1 Multiple functions

```
Worksheet    Query Builder
    1 ⊟ SELECT
    2       product, quantity,
    3       AVG(quantity) OVER(ORDER BY product DESC
    4       ROWS BETWEEN UNBOUNDED PRECEDING
    5       AND CURRENT ROW) caq,
    6       COUNT (*) OVER(ORDER BY product
    7       ROWS BETWEEN UNBOUNDED PRECEDING
    8       AND CURRENT ROW) cnt
    9    FROM
   10       sales;
```

Script Output ×   ▷ Query Result ×

SQL | All Rows Fetched: 10 in 0.015 seconds

	PRODUCT	QUANTITY	CAQ	CNT
1	C	1	5.5	1
2	C++	2	6	2
3	Eclipse	3	6.5	3
4	MongoDB	4	7	4
5	MySQL	5	7.5	5
6	Oracle	6	8	6
7	PostgreSQL	7	8.5	7
8	R	8	9	8
9	RStudio	9	9.5	9
10	SQL	10	10	10

Figure 5-1 Multiple functions

Nesting Functions

You can nest an analytic function into a single-row function. In Example 5-2 below the AVG analytic function is nested under the TRUNC single-row function, which rounds the caq into two decimals.

```
SELECT
  product, sales_date, quantity ,
  AVG(quantity) OVER(ORDER BY sales_date ROWS
  BETWEEN 2 PRECEDING AND CURRENT ROW ) caq,
  TRUNC( AVG(quantity) OVER(ORDER BY
  sales_date ROWS BETWEEN 2 PRECEDING AND CURRENT ROW ) ) trunc_caq
FROM
  sales ;
```

Example 5-2 Nesting function

```
Worksheet    Query Builder
  1 ⊟ SELECT
  2      product, sales_date, quantity ,
  3      AVG(quantity) OVER(ORDER BY sales_date ROWS
  4      BETWEEN 2 PRECEDING AND CURRENT ROW ) caq,
  5      TRUNC( AVG(quantity) OVER(ORDER BY
  6      sales_date ROWS BETWEEN 2 PRECEDING AND CURRENT ROW ) ) trunc_caq
  7    FROM
  8      sales ;
```

Query Result ×

SQL | All Rows Fetched: 10 in 0.427 seconds

	PRODUCT	SALES_DATE	QUANTITY	CAQ	TRUNC_CAQ
1	C	16-06-04	10	10	10
2	MySQL	16-06-04	1	5.5	5
3	PostgreSQL	16-06-04	2	4.3333333333333333333333333333333333333333	4
4	Oracle	16-06-05	3	2	2
5	RStudio	16-06-05	5	3.3333333333333333333333333333333333333333	3
6	R	16-06-05	8	5.3333333333333333333333333333333333333333	5
7	Eclipse	16-06-05	6	6.3333333333333333333333333333333333333333	6
8	C++	16-06-07	9	7.6666666666666666666666666666666666666667	7
9	MongoDB	16-06-09	4	6.3333333333333333333333333333333333333333	6
10	SQL	16-06-10	7	6.6666666666666666666666666666666666666667	6

Figure 5-2 Nesting function

You can also nest a single-row function into an analytic function. In Example 5-3 ROUND is nested under the AVG function.

```
SELECT
  product, sales_date, unit_price,
  AVG(ROUND(unit_price))
  OVER(ORDER BY sales_date
  RANGE BETWEEN 0 PRECEDING AND CURRENT ROW ) rnd_caq
FROM
  Sales;
```

Example 5-3 Single row function nested

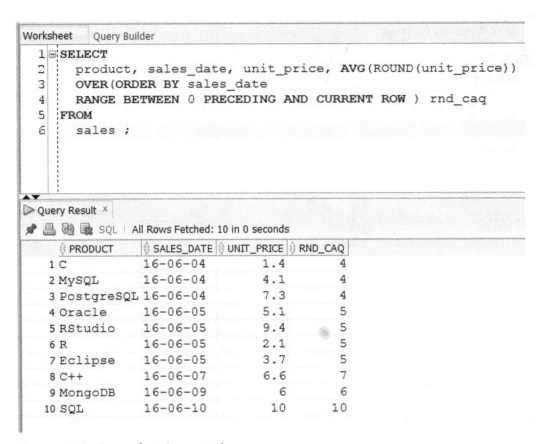

Figure 5-3 Single row function nested

But, nesting non single-row function into an analytic function is not allowed. In the Example 5-4 the query fails trying to nest the COUNT aggregate function into the AVG analytic function.

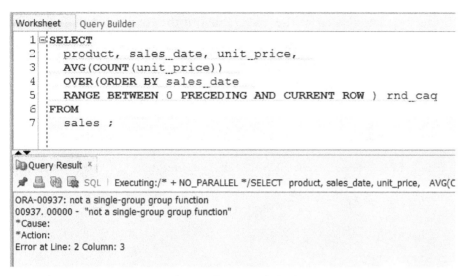

```
1 SELECT
2    product, sales_date, unit_price,
3    AVG(COUNT(unit_price))
4    OVER(ORDER BY sales_date
5    RANGE BETWEEN 0 PRECEDING AND CURRENT ROW ) rnd_caq
6 FROM
7    sales ;
```

Query Result ×

SQL | Executing:/* + NO_PARALLEL */SELECT product, sales_date, unit_price, AVG(C

```
ORA-00937: not a single-group group function
00937. 00000 -  "not a single-group group function"
*Cause:
*Action:
Error at Line: 2 Column: 3
```

Example 5-4 Nesting non-single row function failed

Source Rows

In all previous examples, the rows the AVG function processes (computes the caq) are from a table, the sales table. In Example 5-5, the source rows are the rows returned by the subquery that unionizes two tables.

Suppose we have the following sales history table.

	PRODUCT	QUANTITY	SALES_DATE	CATEGORY
1	C	9	04-JUN-13	Language
2	C++	6	07-JUN-14	Language
3	Eclipse	3	05-JUN-15	IDE
4	MongoDB	10	09-JUN-13	Database
5	MySQL	2	04-JUN-15	Database
6	Oracle	8	05-JUN-13	Database
7	R	5	05-JUN-14	Language
8	RStudio	4	05-JUN-15	IDE
9	SQL	1	04-JUN-11	Database
10	SQL	7	10-JUN-14	Language

In Example 5-5 the rows are also from the sales table but the rows are now ordered by product descending. Notice that ORDER BY is inside the parentheses surrounding the unionized queries. The ORDER BY here orders the source rows for the function; it is not for ordering the query output rows.

```
SELECT
  product, category, quantity,
  AVG(quantity)
  OVER(ORDER BY product
  ROWS BETWEEN 1 PRECEDING AND CURRENT ROW ) rnd_caq
FROM
  (SELECT product, category, quantity
  FROM sales s
  UNION ALL
  SELECT product, category, quantity
  FROM sales_history sh
  WHERE EXTRACT (YEAR FROM sh.sales_date) <= 2014);
```

Example 5-5 Source rows from subquery

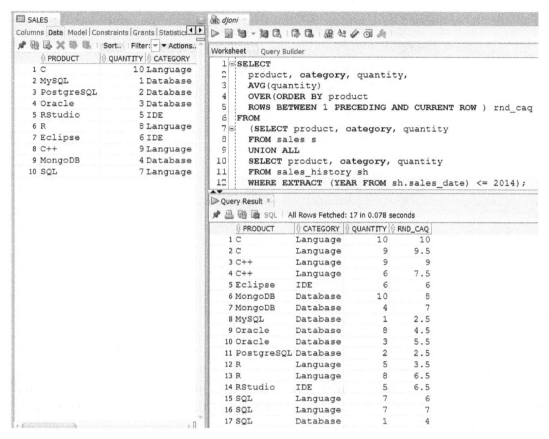

Figure 5-5 Subquery source rows

Aggregated Source Rows

Source rows can be aggregated rows grouped by the GROUP BY clause of the query. Here is an example (Example 5-6)

```
SELECT product, sales_date,
    SUM( SUM(quantity) )
    OVER (PARTITION BY product
ORDER BY product, sales_date ROWS UNBOUNDED
  PRECEDING) AS CUM_SALES
FROM sales s
GROUP BY product,
  sales_date;
```

Example 5-6 Aggregated source rows

The sales table queried by Example 5-6 has two C rows with the same sales date.

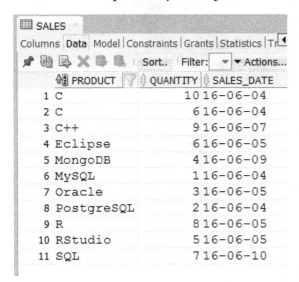

The query requires a nested SUM.

- The inner SUM operates as an aggregate function in conjunction with the GROUP BY clause.
- The outer SUM operates as analytical function. Its source rows are the aggregated rows produced by the inner SUM. Hence, the two C rows are already aggregated into one.

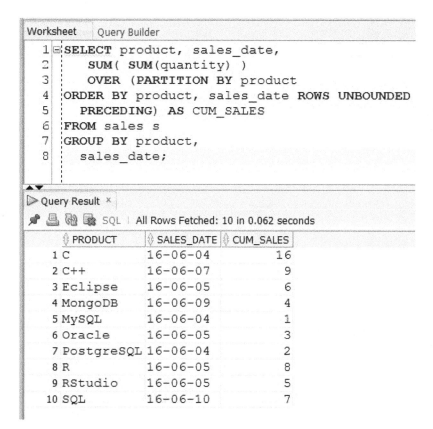

Figure 5-6 Aggregated source rows

The query would fail without the nested SUM.

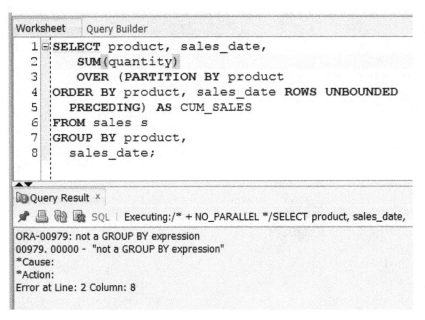

Figure 5-7 Failure without nested SUM

Ordering the Output Rows

You have seen the use of two ORDER BY clauses: In the windowing clause and in the subquery that supplies the source rows.

In Example 5-7, the *ORDER BY sales_date* orders the output rows returned by the query on the sales dates. ORDER BY clause on the query's output is processed at the end, after the analytical function finishes its computation, hence this ODER BY clause does not influence caq computation.

```
SELECT
  product, sales_date, quantity,
  AVG (quantity)
  OVER (ORDER BY sales_date DESC
  RANGE BETWEEN UNBOUNDED PRECEDING
  AND CURRENT ROW) caq, unit_price
FROM sales
ORDER BY unit_price;
----
SELECT
  product, sales_date, quantity,
  AVG (quantity)
  OVER (ORDER BY sales_date DESC
  RANGE BETWEEN UNBOUNDED PRECEDING
  AND CURRENT ROW) caq
FROM sales
ORDER BY product;
```

Example 5-7 Different Order Directions of Output Rows

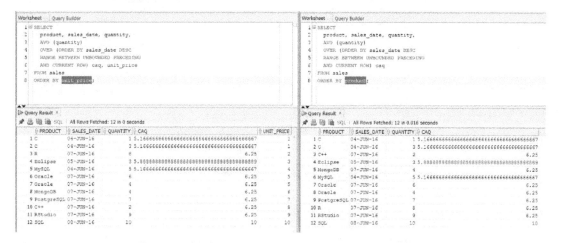

Figure 5-8 ORDER BY of the query does not impact analytic function

In the order clause of the query

In all our examples so far, the analytic functions are in the select list. The only other place you can have analytic function is in the ORDER BY clause of the SELECT statement.

Example 5-8 has a COUNT analytic function in the query's ORDER BY clause. Note that with the OVER clause, the COUNT operates an analytic function here.

- Its order is by unit price.
- Pay attention when interpreting the AVG analytic function in the select list where its order is by product.

```
SELECT
  product, quantity,
  AVG(quantity)
  OVER(ORDER BY product
  ROWS BETWEEN 1 PRECEDING AND CURRENT ROW
  ) caq
  , unit_price
FROM
  sales
  ORDER BY COUNT (*)
  OVER(ORDER BY unit_price DESC);
```

Example 5-8 Analytic function in query's order by clause

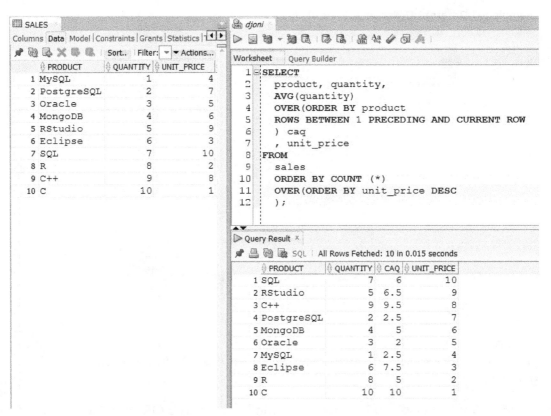

Figure 5-9 Analytic function in query's order by clause

What is Next?

You are now equipped with all that is necessary to look into the individual Oracle supplied analytic functions in the next two chapters.

Chapter 6: Windowing in Aggregate Functions

The five aggregate functions

Table 6-1 lists the five aggregate functions and their purposes.

Function	Purpose
AVG	Compute average
COUNT	Count rows
MAX	Identify maximum
MIN	Identify minimum
SUM	Compute sum

Table 6-1 Aggregate Functions

In each of the next five sections, you will learn the details of the five functions in Table 6-1 as analytic function.

AVG

The AVG function computes average value (arithmetic mean).

Syntax

The AVG function has the following syntax.

```
AVG ([DISTINCT | ALL] expression) [OVER (analytic_clause)]
```

- AVG returns the average of expression, which is the sum of expressions of the window rows divided by the number of the window rows.
- Expression must be numeric or any nonnumeric that can be implicitly converted to numeric.
- The returned data type is the numeric data type of expression.
- The ALL option is the default.

Examples

In Example 6-1 ALL is implied. Note that NULL expression (quantity) is ignored in the calculation of the average.

```
SELECT
  product, sales_date, quantity,
  AVG (quantity)
  OVER(ORDER BY sales_date
    RANGE BETWEEN UNBOUNDED PRECEDING AND CURRENT ROW) caq
FROM sales
ORDER BY sales_date;
```

53

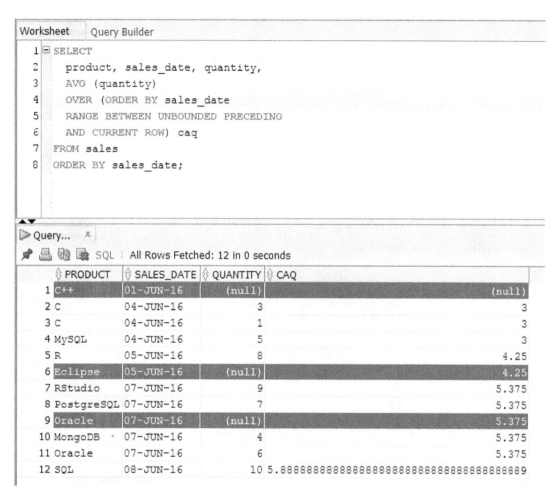

Example 6-1 AVG Function with the ALL default and null expression

Apply DISTINCT if you want to consider duplicates once only, but you cannot apply the order and window clauses, meaning all rows in a partition gets the same average. See Example 6-2 for an example.

```
SELECT
  product, category, quantity,
  AVG (DISTINCT quantity)
  OVER(PARTITION BY category) caq
FROM sales
ORDER BY category;
```

```
Worksheet    Query Builder
  1  SELECT
  2    product, category, quantity,
  3    AVG (DISTINCT quantity)
  4    OVER(PARTITION BY category) caq
  5  FROM sales
  6  ORDER BY category;
```

▷ Query Result ✕

📌 🖨 🔁 🔻 SQL | All Rows Fetched: 12 in 0 seconds

	PRODUCT	CATEGORY	QUANTITY	CAQ
1	MySQL	Database	4	6
2	MongoDB	Database	4	6
3	Oracle	Database	6	6
4	PostgreSQL	Database	8	6
5	Oracle	Database	(null)	6
6	RStudio	IDE	9	9
7	Eclipse	IDE	(null)	9
8	C	Language	1	5.5
9	C	Language	3	5.5
10	R	Language	8	5.5
11	SQL	Language	10	5.5
12	C++	Language	(null)	5.5

Example 6-2 DISTINCT argument

COUNT

The COUNT function computes average value (arithmetic mean).

Syntax

The COUNT function has the following syntax.

```
COUNT({ * | [ DISTINCT | ALL ] expr }) [ OVER (analytic_clause) ]
```

COUNT has the same syntax as AVG, except the * argument option. If you specify the asterisk (*), then this function returns all rows, including duplicates and nulls.

Example

```
SELECT
  product, sales_date,
  COUNT (*)
  OVER(ORDER BY sales_date
     RANGE BETWEEN CURRENT ROW AND CURRENT ROW) caq
FROM sales
ORDER BY sales_date;
----

----------------------------------------------------------
--  File created - Tuesday-August-02-2016
----------------------------------------------------------
REM INSERTING into SALES
SET DEFINE OFF;
Insert into SALES (PRODUCT,QUANTITY,SALES_DATE,UNIT_PRICE,CATEGORY)
      values ('C++',null,to_date('01-JUN-16','DD-MON-RR'),8,'Language');
Insert into SALES (PRODUCT,QUANTITY,SALES_DATE,UNIT_PRICE,CATEGORY)
      values ('C',3,to_date('04-JUN-16','DD-MON-RR'),1,'Language');
Insert into SALES (PRODUCT,QUANTITY,SALES_DATE,UNIT_PRICE,CATEGORY)
      values ('C',3,to_date('04-JUN-16','DD-MON-RR'),1,'Language');
Insert into SALES (PRODUCT,QUANTITY,SALES_DATE,UNIT_PRICE,CATEGORY)
      values ('MySQL',4,to_date('04-JUN-16','DD-MON-RR'),4,'Database');
Insert into SALES (PRODUCT,QUANTITY,SALES_DATE,UNIT_PRICE,CATEGORY)
      values (null,8,to_date('05-JUN-16','DD-MON-RR'),2,'Language');
Insert into SALES (PRODUCT,QUANTITY,SALES_DATE,UNIT_PRICE,CATEGORY)
      values ('Eclipse',null,to_date('05-JUN-16','DD-MON-RR'),3,'IDE');
Insert into SALES (PRODUCT,QUANTITY,SALES_DATE,UNIT_PRICE,CATEGORY)
      values ('PostgreSQL',8,to_date('07-JUN-16','DD-MON-
      RR'),7,'Database');
```

```
Insert into SALES (PRODUCT,QUANTITY,SALES_DATE,UNIT_PRICE,CATEGORY)
      values ('Oracle',3,to_date('07-JUN-16','DD-MON-RR'),5,'Database');
Insert into SALES (PRODUCT,QUANTITY,SALES_DATE,UNIT_PRICE,CATEGORY)
      values ('Oracle',4,to_date('07-JUN-16','DD-MON-RR'),6,'Database');
Insert into SALES (PRODUCT,QUANTITY,SALES_DATE,UNIT_PRICE,CATEGORY)
      values ('Oracle',6,to_date('07-JUN-16','DD-MON-RR'),5,'Database');
Insert into SALES (PRODUCT,QUANTITY,SALES_DATE,UNIT_PRICE,CATEGORY)
      values ('RStudio',9,null,9,'IDE');
Insert into SALES (PRODUCT,QUANTITY,SALES_DATE,UNIT_PRICE,CATEGORY)
      values ('SQL',10,null,10,'Language');
----
```

Worksheet | Query Builder

```
1 SELECT
2   product, sales_date,
3   COUNT (*)
4   OVER(ORDER BY sales_date
5      RANGE BETWEEN CURRENT ROW AND CURRENT ROW) caq
6 FROM sales
7 ORDER BY sales_date;
```

Query Result ×

SQL | All Rows Fetched: 12 in 0 seconds

	PRODUCT	SALES_DATE	CAQ
1	C++	01-JUN-16	1
2	C	04-JUN-16	3
3	C	04-JUN-16	3
4	MySQL	04-JUN-16	3
5	(null)	05-JUN-16	2
6	Eclipse	05-JUN-16	2
7	PostgreSQL	07-JUN-16	4
8	Oracle	07-JUN-16	4
9	Oracle	07-JUN-16	4
10	Oracle	07-JUN-16	4
11	RStudio	(null)	2
12	SQL	(null)	2

Example 6-4 The * argument

The same as AVG, COUNT with DISTINCT does not consider null and duplicates are counted only once. Example 6-... demonstrates these behaviours.

```
SELECT
  product, category, quantity,
  COUNT (DISTINCT product)
  OVER(partition by category) cntq
FROM sales
ORDER BY category, product;
```

Worksheet	Query Builder

```
1 ☐ SELECT
2     product, category, quantity,
3     COUNT (DISTINCT product)
4     OVER(partition by category) cntq
5   FROM sales
6   ORDER BY category, product;
```

▲▼

▷ Query Result ×

📌 🖨 🔧 📑 SQL | All Rows Fetched: 12 in 0 seconds

	PRODUCT	CATEGORY	QUANTITY	CNTQ
1	MySQL	Database	4	3
2	Oracle	Database	6	3
3	Oracle	Database	3	3
4	Oracle	Database	4	3
5	PostgreSQL	Database	8	3
6	Eclipse	IDE	(null)	2
7	RStudio	IDE	9	2
8	C	Language	1	3
9	C	Language	3	3
10	C++	Language	(null)	3
11	SQL	Language	10	3
12	(null)	Language	8	3

Example 6-5 DISTINCT argument

COUNT never returns null as shown in Example 6-6. The first row (C++ row) does not have any preceding row and its quantity is null. As null is not counted, this row does not have any row to be counted, the function returns 0, not null.

```
SELECT
  product, quantity, sales_date,
  COUNT (quantity)
  OVER(PARTITION BY sales_date ORDER BY sales_date
    RANGE BETWEEN 1 PRECEDING AND CURRENT ROW) cntaq
FROM sales
ORDER BY sales_date;
```

Worksheet	Query Builder

```
1 ⊟ SELECT
2      product, quantity, sales_date,
3      COUNT (quantity)
4      OVER(PARTITION BY sales_date ORDER BY sales_date
5          RANGE BETWEEN 1 PRECEDING AND CURRENT ROW) cntaq
6    FROM sales
7    ORDER BY sales_date;
```

▶ Query Result ×

📌 🖨 🔊 📑 SQL | All Rows Fetched: 12 in 0 seconds

	PRODUCT	QUANTITY	SALES_DATE	CNTAQ
1	C++	(null)	01-JUN-16	0
2	C	3	04-JUN-16	3
3	C	3	04-JUN-16	3
4	MySQL	4	04-JUN-16	3
5	(null)	8	05-JUN-16	1
6	Eclipse	(null)	05-JUN-16	1
7	PostgreSQL	8	07-JUN-16	4
8	Oracle	3	07-JUN-16	4
9	Oracle	4	07-JUN-16	4
10	Oracle	6	07-JUN-16	4
11	RStudio	9	(null)	2
12	SQL	10	(null)	2

Example 6-6 COUNT never returns null

MAX

The MAX function returns the maximum value of expression.

Syntax

The MAX syntax is:

```
MAX ([DISTINCT | ALL] expr) [OVER (analytic_clause)]
```

You might have noticed that MAX has the same syntax as the AVG's.

Example

Example 6-7 returns the maximum sale amount among rows of the same sales date.

```
SELECT product,
  category,
  quantity,
  unit_price,
  (quantity * unit_price) sale_amt,
  sales_date,
  MAX(quantity * unit_price)
  OVER (PARTITION BY category
  ORDER BY (sales_date)  DESC
  RANGE BETWEEN CURRENT ROW AND 2 FOLLOWING ) max_sale_amt
FROM sales;
```

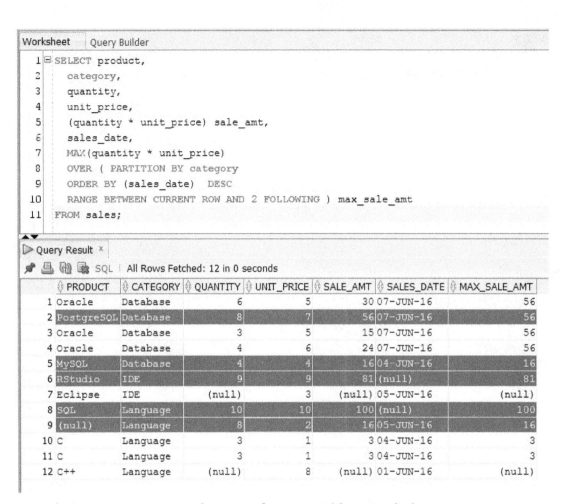

Example 6-7 MAX returns max sale amount from rows with same sale date

MIN

The MIN function returns the minimum value of expression.

Syntax

The MIN syntax is:

```
MIN ([DISTINCT | ALL] expr) [OVER (analytic_clause)]
```

You might have noticed that MAX has the same syntax as the MIN's.

Example

MIN is the same as MAX except that returns minimum value instead of max. Example 6-8 returns the miminumsale amount among rows of the same sales date.

```
SELECT product, category, quantity, unit_price,
  (quantity * unit_price) sales_amt, sales_date,
  MIN(quantity * unit_price)
  OVER
  (PARTITION BY category
    ORDER BY (sales_date)
    RANGE UNBOUNDED PRECEDING
    ) min_sale_amt
FROM sales;
```

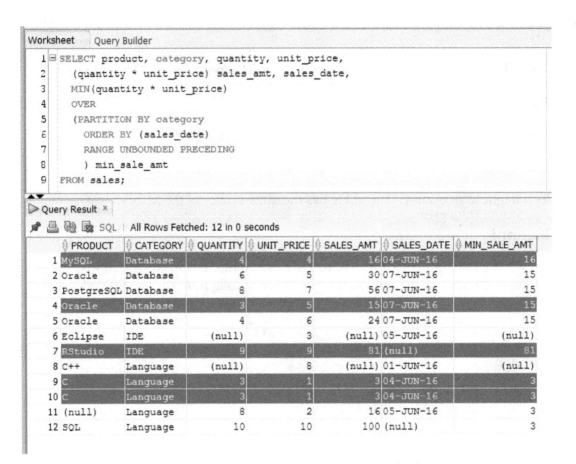

Example 6-8 MAX returns max sale amount from rows with same sale date

SUM

The SUM function computes the sum of values (total values).

Syntax

```
SUM([ DISTINCT | ALL ] expression) OVER (analytic_clause) ]
```

- SUM returns the sum of expressions of the window rows
- Expression must be numeric or any nonnumeric that can be implicitly converted to numeric.
- The returned data type is the numeric data type of expression.
- The ALL option is the default.

Example

In Example 6-9 the analytic SUM function accumulates sales amount (quantity * price) over time.

```
SELECT product, category, sales_dt,
  (quantity * price),
  SUM(quantity * price)
  OVER(PARTITION BY category
  ORDER BY sales_dt, product
  ROWS BETWEEN UNBOUNDED PRECEDING AND CURRENT ROW)
  AS csa
FROM sales;
```

```
Worksheet    Query Builder
 1 ⊟ SELECT product,
 2     category,
 3     sales_date,
 4     quantity ,
 5     unit_price,
 6     (quantity    * unit_price),
 7     SUM(quantity * unit_price)
 8     OVER(PARTITION BY category ORDER BY sales_date,
 9     product ROWS BETWEEN UNBOUNDED PRECEDING AND CURRENT ROW) AS csa
10   FROM sales;
```

Query Result ×

SQL | All Rows Fetched: 12 in 0 seconds

	PRODUCT	CATEGORY	SALES_DATE	QUANTITY	UNIT_PRICE	(QUANTITY*UNIT_PRICE)	CSA
1	MySQL	Database	04-JUN-16	4	4	16	16
2	Oracle	Database	07-JUN-16	6	5	30	46
3	Oracle	Database	07-JUN-16	3	5	15	61
4	Oracle	Database	07-JUN-16	4	6	24	85
5	PostgreSQL	Database	07-JUN-16	8	7	56	141
6	Eclipse	IDE	05-JUN-16	(null)	3	(null)	(null)
7	RStudio	IDE	(null)	9	9	81	81
8	C++	Language	01-JUN-16	(null)	8	(null)	(null)
9	C	Language	04-JUN-16	3	1	3	3
10	C	Language	04-JUN-16	3	1	3	6
11	(null)	Language	05-JUN-16	8	2	16	22
12	SQL	Language	(null)	10	10	100	122

Chapter 7: FIRST_VALUE, LAST_VALUE and NTH_VALUE functions

The next three analytic functions you will learn in this final chapter identify a window row that have the first or last, or a specific value.

FIRST_VALUE

FIRST_VALUE identifies the value of the first row in a window.

Syntax

The syntax of the analytic FIRST_VALUE function is:

```
FIRST_VALUE (expression)
   [{RESPECT | IGNORE} NULLS]
   OVER (analytic_clause)
```

- FIRST_VALUE returns the *expression* of the first row in a window.
- {RESPECT | IGNORE} NULLS determines whether null of `expression` is included in or eliminated from the calculation.
  - o The default is RESPECT NULLS, which returns NULL if the first value is NULL.
  - o IGNORE NULLS, returns the first non-null value in the set, or NULL if all values in the window are null.

Example

Here's an example with two FIRST_VALUE functions, one respecting nulls and nulls first; the other ignoring nulls.

```
SELECT
  product,category, quantity, unit_price,(quantity*unit_price) sales_amt,
  FIRST_VALUE ( quantity * unit_price)
  OVER(PARTITION BY category
  ORDER BY (quantity * unit_price) NULLS FIRST
  RANGE BETWEEN UNBOUNDED PRECEDING AND CURRENT ROW) AS fv
  , FIRST_VALUE( quantity * unit_price)
  IGNORE NULLS
  OVER(PARTITION BY category
```

```
ORDER BY (quantity * unit_price)
  RANGE BETWEEN UNBOUNDED PRECEDING AND CURRENT ROW) AS ignr
FROM
  sales;
```

Example 7-1 FIRST_VALUE

```
Worksheet    Query Builder
 1  SELECT
 2    product,category, quantity, unit_price,(quantity*unit_price) sales_amt,
 3    FIRST_VALUE ( quantity * unit_price)
 4    OVER(PARTITION BY category
 5    ORDER BY --product --
 6    (quantity * unit_price) NULLS FIRST
 7    RANGE BETWEEN UNBOUNDED PRECEDING AND CURRENT ROW) AS fv
 8    , FIRST_VALUE( quantity * unit_price)
 9    IGNORE NULLS
10    OVER(PARTITION BY category
11    ORDER BY --product --
12    (quantity * unit_price)
13    RANGE BETWEEN UNBOUNDED PRECEDING AND CURRENT ROW) AS ignr
14  FROM
15    sales;
```

Query Result ×

SQL | All Rows Fetched: 12 in 0.016 seconds

	PRODUCT	CATEGORY	QUANTITY	UNIT_PRICE	SALES_AMT	FV	IGNR
1	Oracle	Database	3	5	15	15	15
2	MySQL	Database	4	4	16	15	15
3	Oracle	Database	4	6	24	15	15
4	Oracle	Database	6	5	30	15	15
5	PostgreSQL	Database	8	7			
6	Eclipse	IDE	3	3			
7	RStudio	IDE	9	9	81	9	9
8	C++	Language	(null)	8	(null)	(null)	3
9	C	Language	3	1	3	(null)	3
10	C	Language	3	1	3	(null)	3
11	(null)	Language	8	2	16	(null)	3
12	SQL	Language	10	10	100	(null)	3

respect nulls (default) and nulls first

Ignore nulls, so take3

Figure 7-1 FIRST_VALUE

LAST_VALUE

LAST_VALUE identifies the value of the last row in a window

Syntax

The syntax of the analytic LAST_VALUE function is:

```
LASTST_VALUE (expression)
  [{RESPECT | IGNORE} NULLS]
  OVER (analytic_clause)
```

- LAST_VALUE returns the *expression* value of the last row in a window.
- {RESPECT | IGNORE} NULLS determines whether null values of `expression` are included in or eliminated from the calculation.
  - The default is RESPECT NULLS, which returns NULL if the last value is NULL.
  - IGNORE NULLS, returns the last non-null value in the set, or NULL if all values in the window are null.

Example

Here is an example.

```
SELECT
  product,category, quantity, unit_price,
  (quantity*unit_price) sales_amt,
  LAST_VALUE ( quantity * unit_price)
  OVER(PARTITION BY category
  ORDER BY (quantity * unit_price)
  ROWS BETWEEN 2 PRECEDING AND 2 FOLLOWING) AS fv
  , LAST_VALUE( quantity * unit_price)
  IGNORE NULLS
  OVER(PARTITION BY category
  ORDER BY (quantity * unit_price)
  ROWS BETWEEN 2 PRECEDING AND 2 FOLLOWING) AS ignr
FROM
  Sales;
```

Example 7-2 LAST_VALUE

68

```
Worksheet   Query Builder
 1  SELECT
 2    product,category, quantity, unit_price,
 3    (quantity*unit_price) sales_amt,
 4    LAST_VALUE ( quantity * unit_price)
 5    OVER(PARTITION BY category
 6    ORDER BY (quantity * unit_price)
 7    ROWS BETWEEN 2 PRECEDING AND 2 FOLLOWING) AS fv
 8    , LAST_VALUE( quantity * unit_price)
 9    IGNORE NULLS
10    OVER(PARTITION BY category
11    ORDER BY (quantity * unit_price)
12    ROWS BETWEEN 2 PRECEDING AND 2 FOLLOWING) AS ignr
13  FROM
14    sales;
```

Query Result ×

SQL | All Rows Fetched: 12 in 0 seconds

	PRODUCT	CATEGORY	QUANTITY	UNIT_PRICE	SALES_AMT	FV	IGNR
1	Oracle	Database	3	5	15	24	24
2	MySQL	Database	4	4	16	30	30
3	Oracle	Database	4	6	24	56	56
4	Oracle	Database	6	5	30	56	56
5	PostgreSQL	Database	8	7	56	56	56
6	Eclipse	IDE	3	3	9	81	81
7	RStudio	IDE	9	9	81	81	81
8	C	Language	3	1	3	16	16
9	C	Language	3	1	3	100	100
10	(null)	Language	8	2	16	(null)	100
11	SQL	Language	10	10	100	(null)	100
12	C++	Language	(null)	8	(null)	(null)	100

Figure 7-2 LAST_VALUE

NTH_VALUE

The `NTH_VALUE` function returns a value of the *n*th row.

Syntax

```
NTH_VALUE (expression, n)
  [FROM {FIRST | LAST }]
  [{RESPECT | IGNORE } NULLS]
  OVER (analytic_clause)
```

The returned value has the data type of the *measure_expr*.

- {RESPECT | IGNORE} NULLS determines whether null values of *expression* is included in or eliminated from the calculation. The default is RESPECTNULLS.
- *n* determines the *n*th row for which the measure value is to be returned. *n* can be a constant, bind variable, column, or an expression involving them, as long as it resolves to a positive integer. The function returns NULL if the data source window has fewer than *n* rows. If *n* is null, then the function returns an error.
- FROM {FIRST | LAST} determines whether the calculation begins at the first or last row of the window. The default is FROM FIRST.

Example

Example 7-3 uses the NTH_VALUE function, which identifies the 3rd values in a window. Windows that have less than 3 rows get null.

```
SELECT
  product,category, quantity, unit_price,
  (quantity*unit_price) sales_amt,
  NTH_VALUE ( quantity * unit_price, 3) -- 3rd value
  OVER(PARTITION BY category
  ORDER BY (quantity * unit_price)
  ROWS BETWEEN 1 PRECEDING AND 2 FOLLOWING) AS nth
FROM
  sales;
```

Example 7-3 3RD_VALUE

Worksheet | Query Builder

```
1 ⊟SELECT
2     product,category, quantity, unit_price,
3     (quantity*unit_price) sales_amt,
4     NTH_VALUE ( quantity * unit_price, 3) -- 3rd value
5     OVER(PARTITION BY category
6     ORDER BY (quantity * unit_price)
7     ROWS BETWEEN 1 PRECEDING AND 2 FOLLOWING) AS nth
8  FROM
9     sales;
```

▶ Query Result ×

📌 🖨 🔟 🔟 SQL | All Rows Fetched: 12 in 0.016 seconds

	PRODUCT	CATEGORY	QUANTITY	UNIT_PRICE	SALES_AMT	NTH
1	Oracle	Database	3	5	15	24
2	MySQL	Database	4	4	16	24
3	Oracle	Database	4	6	24	30
4	Oracle	Database	6	5	30	56
5	PostgreSQL	Database	8	7	56	(null)
6	Eclipse	IDE	3	3	9	(null)
7	RStudio	IDE	9	9	81	(null)
8	C	Language	3	1	3	16
9	C	Language	3	1	3	16
10	(null)	Language	8	2	16	100
11	SQL	Language	10	10	100	(null)
12	C++	Language	(null)	8	(null)	(null)

Figure 7-3 Third_VALUE

Appendix A: Setting Up

This first chapter is a guide to install and set up the Oracle Database 11g Expression Edition release 2 and SQL Developer version 4. Both are available at the Oracle website for download at no charge.

Installing Database Express Edition

Go to http://www.oracle.com/technetwork/indexes/downloads/index.html

Locate and download the Windows version of the Oracle Database Express Edition (XE). You will be requested to accept the license agreement. If you don't have one, create an account; it's free.

Unzip the downloaded file to a folder in your local drive, and then, double-click the setup.exe file.

You will see the Welcome window.

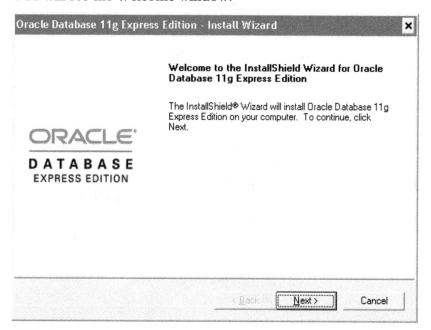

Click the Next> button, accept the agreement on the License Agreement window, and then click the Next> button again.

The next window is the "Choose Destination Location" window.

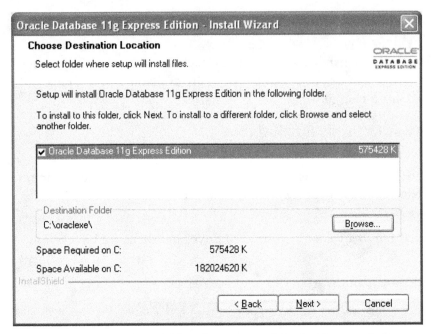

Accept the destination folder shown, or click the Browse button to choose a different folder for your installation, and then click the Next> button.

On the prompt for port numbers, accept the defaults, and then click the Next> button.

On the Passwords window, enter a password of your choice and confirm it, and then click the Next> button. The SYS and SYSTEM accounts created during this installation are for the database operation and administration, respectively. Note the password; you will use the SYSTEM account and its password for creating your own account, which you use for trying the examples.

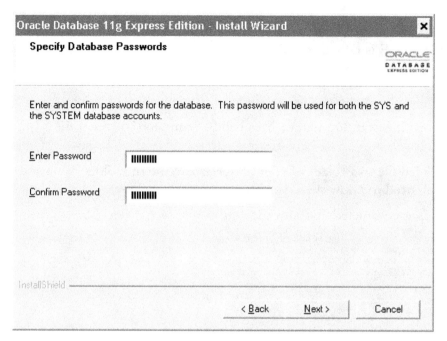

The Summary window will be displayed. Click Install.

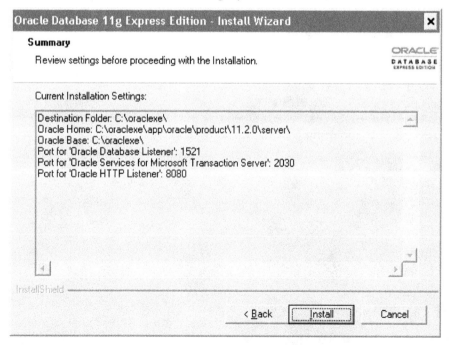

Finally, when the Installation Completion window appears, click the Finish button.

Your Oracle Database XE is now installed.

Installing SQL Developer

Go to http://www.oracle.com/technetwork/indexes/downloads/index.html

Locate and download the SQL Developer. You will be requested to accept the license agreement. If you don't have one, create an account; it's free.

Unzip the downloaded file to a folder of your preference. Note the folder name and its location; you will need to know them to start your SQL Developer.

When the unzipping is completed, look for the sqldeveloper.exe file.

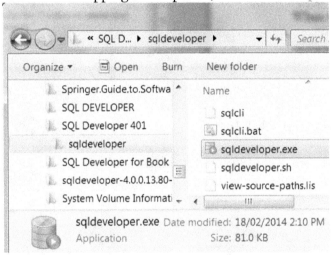

You start SQL Developer by opening (double-clicking) this file.

You might want to create a short-cut on your Desktop.

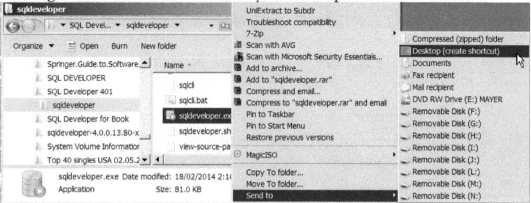

You can then start your SQL Developer by double-clicking the short-cut.

Your initial screen should look like the following. If you don't want to see the Start Page tab the next time you start SQL Developer, un-check the *Show on Startup* box at the bottom left side of the screen.

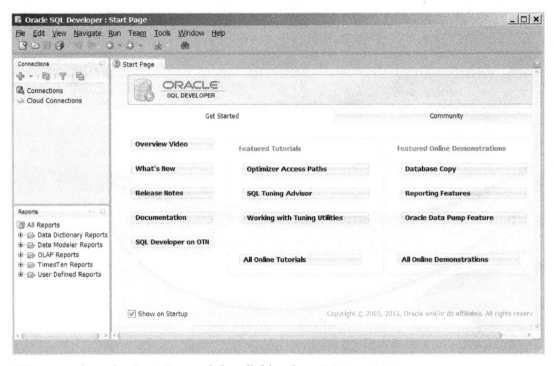

For now, close the Start Page tab by clicking its x.

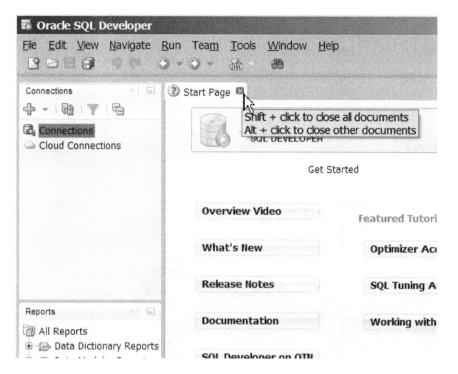

Creating Connection

To work with a database from SQL Developer, you need to have a connection.

A connection is specific to an account. As we will use the SYSTEM account to create your own account, you first have to create a connection for the SYSTEM account.

To create a connection, right-click the Connection folder.

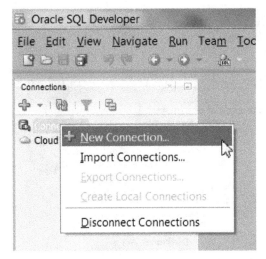

On the New/Select Database Connection window, enter a Connection Name and Username as shown. The Password is the password of SYSTEM account you entered during the Oracle database installation. Check the Save Password box.

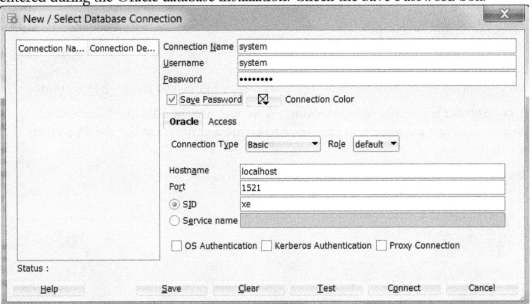

When you click the Connect button, the *system* connection you have just created should be available on the Connection Navigator.

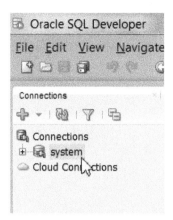

A Worksheet is opened for the system connection. The Worksheet is where you type in source codes.

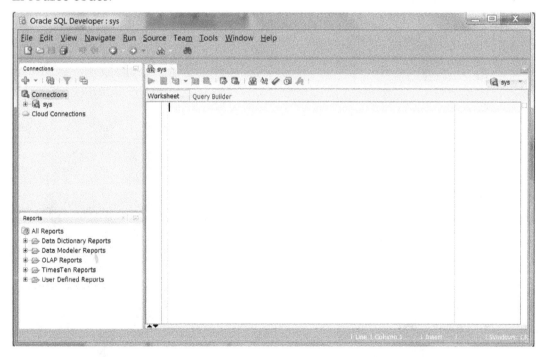

Creating Database Account

You will use your own database account (user) to try the book examples.

To create a new account, expand the system connection and locate the Other Users folder at the bottom of the folder tree.

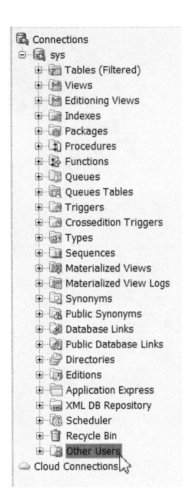

Right click and select Create User.

Enter a User Name of your choice, a password and its confirmation, and then click the Apply button. You should get a successful pop-up window; close it.

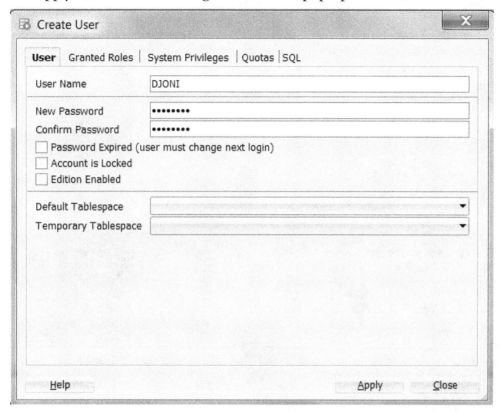

On the Granted Roles tab, click Grant All, Admin All and Default All buttons; then click the Apply button. Close the successful window and the Edit User as well.

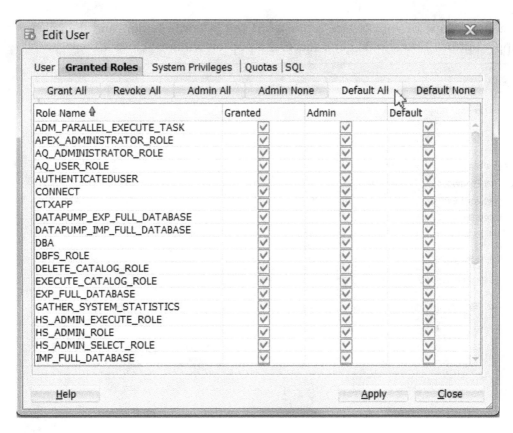

Creating Your Connection

Similar to when you created system connection earlier, now create a connection for your account.

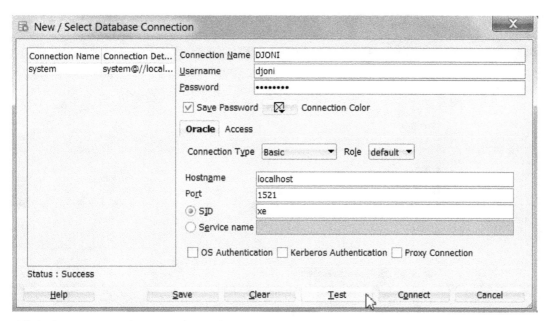

Click the Connect button. A worksheet for your connection is opened (which is *DJONI* in my case).

84

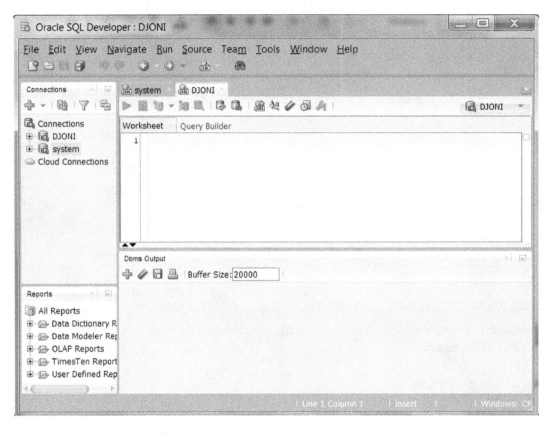

Showing Line Numbers

In describing the book examples I sometimes refer to the line numbers of the program; these are line numbers on the worksheet. To show line numbers, click Preferences from the Tools menu.

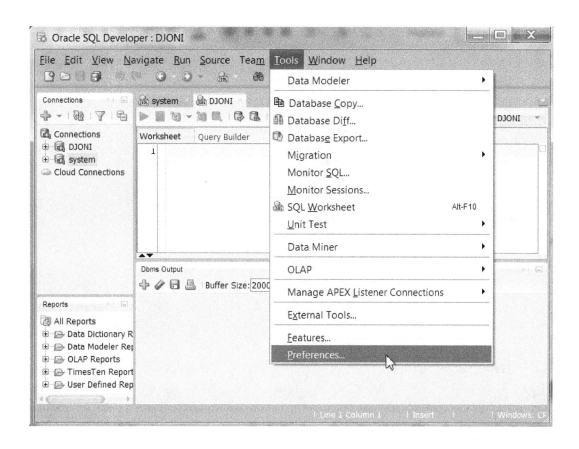

Select Line Gutter, then check the Show Line Numbers. Your Preferences should look like the following. Click the OK button.

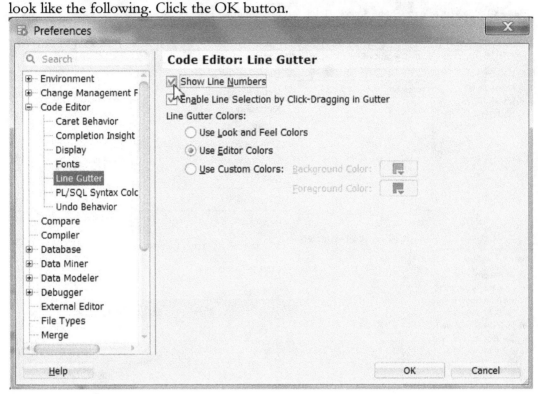

Deleting the *system* Connection

Delete the *system* connection, making sure you don't use this account mistakenly. Click Yes when you are prompted to confirm the deletion. Your SQL Developer is now set.

87

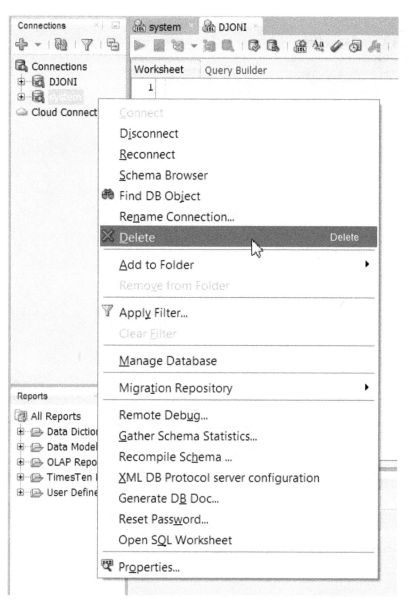

Close the *system* worksheet.

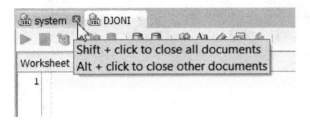

Appendix B: Using SQL Developer

This chapter shows you how to use the SQL Developer features that you will use to try the book examples.

Entering SQL statement

The worksheet is where you enter SQL statement.

Start your SQL Developer if you have not done so. To open a worksheet for your connection, click the + (folder expansion) or double-click the connection name. Alternatively, right-click the connection and click Connect.

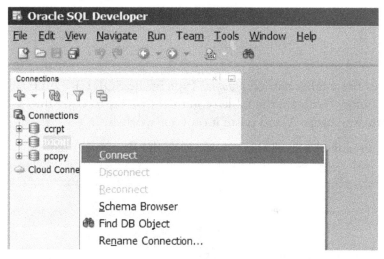

Note the name of the worksheet (tab label) is the name of your connection.

You can type source code on the worksheet.

Appendix A has the source code of all the book examples. Instead of typing, you can copy a source code and paste it on the worksheet.

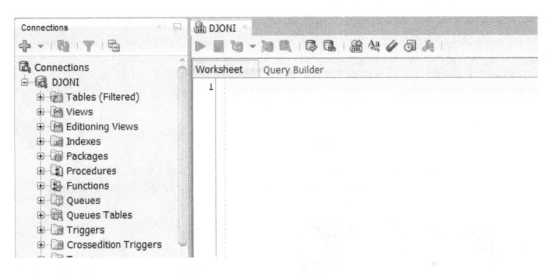

SQL Statement

Some of the book examples use a table named *produce*. Type in the SQL CREATE TABLE statement shown below to create the table (you might prefer to copy the *create_produce.sql* listing from Appendix A and paste it on your worksheet)

You run a SQL statement already in a worksheet by clicking the Run Statement button.

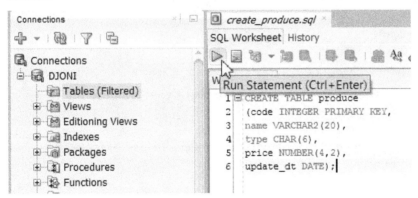

The Script Output pane confirms that the table has been created, and you should see the produce table in the Connection Navigator under your connection folder. If you don't see the newly created table, click Refresh.

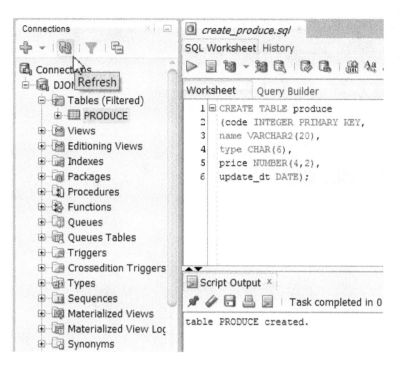

Inserting Rows

As an example of running multiple SQL statements in SQL Developer, the following five statements insert five rows into the produce table. Please type the statements, or copy it from *insert_produce.sql* in Appendix A. You will use these rows when you try the book examples.

Run all statements by clicking the Run Script button, or Ctrl+Enter (press and hold Ctrl button then click Enter button)

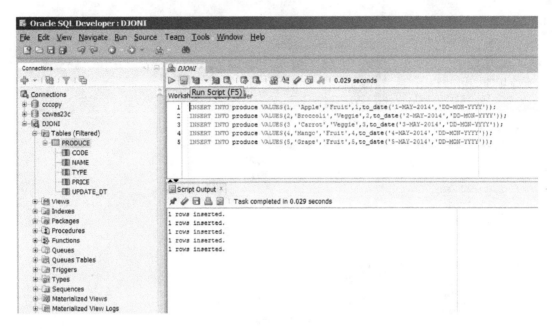

Multiple worksheets for a connection

Sometimes you need to have two or more programs on different worksheets. You can open more than one worksheet for a connection by right-clicking the connection and select Open SQL Worksheet.

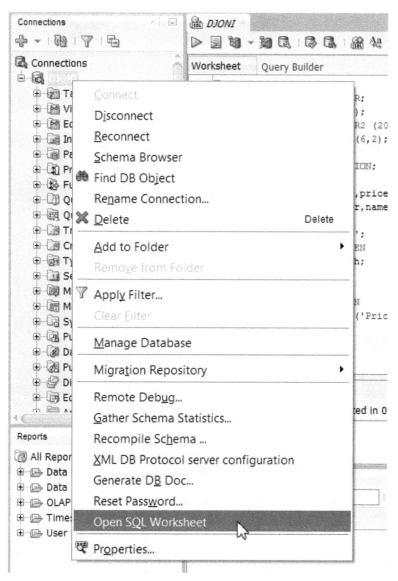

The names of the next tabs for a connection have sequential numbers added.

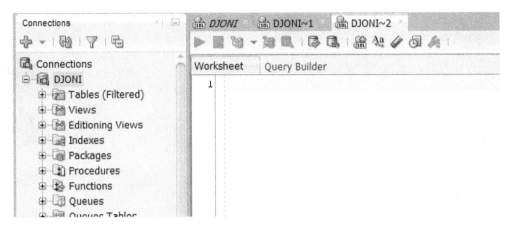

Storing the source code

You can store a source code into a text file for later re-opening by selecting Save from the File menu.

Select the location where you want to store the source code and give the file a name, and then click Save.

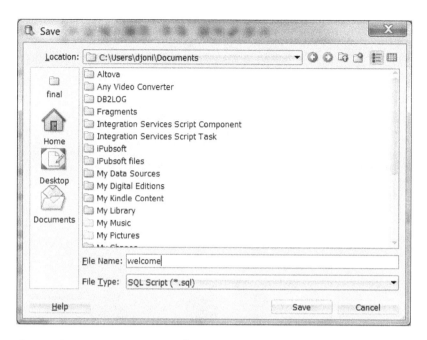

Opening a source code

You can open a source code by selecting Open or Reopen from the File menu and then select the file that contains the source code.

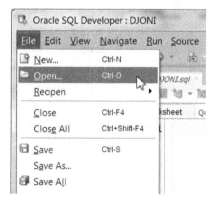

The source code will be opened on a new worksheet. The tab of the worksheet has the name of the file. The following is the worksheet opened for the source code stored as file named running_plsql.sql.

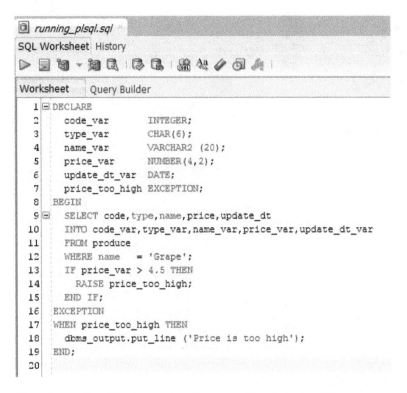

Storing the listings in Appendix A into files

As an alternative to copy and paste, you can store each of the listing into a file and then you can open the file. Note that you must store each program source code into a file.

Running SQL from a file

You can execute a file that contains SQL statement without opening it on the worksheet as shown here.

Clearing a Worksheet
To clear a Worksheet, click its Clear button.

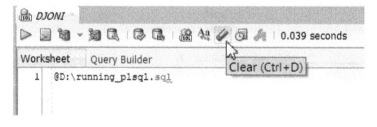

Index

www.ingramcontent.com/pod-product-compliance
Lightning Source LLC
Chambersburg PA
CBHW080557060326
40689CB00021B/4883